Dot and Dash

Written by Susan Frame
Illustrated by Denise Damanti

a Capstone company — publishers for children

Chapter 1

One summer morning, Ella Parker was in her garden shed at number 4 Pepper Road. She was checking on her seedlings. Dot, a red bug, was in Ella's back garden.

"I am in luck!" said Dot. "Ella has a lemon muffin waiting for her in that box by her deck chair. And the lid is up. Lemon muffin for me!"

"But I will have to be quick," said Dot. "I can hear Dash. And that muffin is all for me!"

"Yoo-hoo, Dot! Is that you?" said Dash, as he sat down. "How are you on this hot summer morning?"
But Dot did not look at Dash. She darted down to the muffin.

Dash darted down, too, and sat by Dot. "There is a lot of lemon muffin, there, Dot. Can I have a bit?" he said.
"No," said Dot. "You cannot have a bit. It is all for me. Now, buzz off!"

Dash was sad. "I am too old to buzz," he said with a deep sigh. "But I might see you at noon." And he dashed off high into the air.

Chapter 2

At noon, Dot was at number 6 Pepper Road. She was in Ann Ling's sun room. Ann was sitting with her cat on her lap. She had a thick bit of jam tart on a dish.

"I am in luck! Ann has jam tart on that dish," said Dot. "Oh no, I can hear Dash! I will have to rush."

"Yoo-hoo, Dot! Is that you?" said Dash, as he darted into Ann's sun room. But Dot turned her back on Dash. She rushed down to the jam tart.

"There is so much jam tart there, Dot. Be a good pal and let me have a bit, too," said Dash.

But Dot said, "No, I will not be a good pal. This jam tart is all for me. Now, buzz off!"

"I am too old to buzz, Dot," said Dash with a deep sigh. "Oh well, I might see you tonight."
And he dashed off high into the air.

Chapter 3

That night at number 8 Pepper Road, Jim Hopper was chopping carrots and turnips. He laid the food on a sheet of tin foil.

"I think I will have a short rock in my rocking chair until I have my dinner," he said.

"Yum!" Dot said, licking her lips. "I am in luck. Jim is rocking. And he is cooking carrots and turnips for his dinner. But I will have them for **my** dinner!"

Then Dot said, "I think I can hear Dash. That food is all for me, so I have to be quick!"

"Yoo-hoo, Dot! Are you there?" said Dash, as he rushed in.
But Dot did not look at Dash. She ran up to the carrots and turnips.

Dash sat on the carpet. "There you are!" he said. "You have a lot of food there, Dot. Let's be pals. Can I have a bit?" But Dot turned her back on Dash. "No! I do not need a pal. And you cannot have my carrots and turnips. Buzz off!"

"I think we all need a pal, Dot," Dash sighed. "And I am too old to buzz." All of a sudden there was barking. "Woof! Woof!"

Dot got such a shock. She shot out of the room.
"Oh dear! I forgot the dogs," said Jim, hopping out of his chair. "The dogs need to be fed, too!"
He ran out of the room, as well.

Chapter 4

Dot had not got far. She was on Jim's porch. She did not look well. "Oh, I feel sick. I have had far too much food," she said. "I think I will curl up in this boot and have a short nap until I feel better."

Jim was on the porch, too.
"On with my boots and then I can feed the dogs," he said.
Dash had seen Dot go into Jim's boot.
"Oh no!" he said. "It's up to me to get Dot out of there. I might be too old to buzz, but I am not too old to be a pal!"

Dash sat on the rim of the boot and looked down at Dot.
"Dot!" he yelled. "No napping now. You have to get out!"
"But I feel too ill, Dash," Dot said.

Dash zoomed down to the bottom of the boot. "Hop on my back and hang on tight," he said.

Dot did as he said. Then, up and off they dashed, high into the night air.

That night, the pair sat in the light of the moon. Dot sighed. "I have not been good to you, Dash, but you have been good to me," she said. "Can we be pals?"

"Yes, Dot. We all need a pal," Dash said to her.
"You are so right, Dash. Thank you for bee-ing there for me!" said Dot.